Jean Andrews was born and grew up in the West of Ireland. A poet and translator of poetry, she teaches at the Department of Spanish, Portuguese and Latin American Studies at the University of Nottingham, UK.

Lunatica

Jean Andrews

Published 2013 by arima publishing

www.arimapublishing.com

ISBN 978 1 84549 584 8

© Jean Andrews 2013

All rights reserved

This book is copyright. Subject to statutory exception and to provisions of relevant collective licensing agreements, no part of this publication may be reproduced, stored in a retrieval system, or transmitted in any form or by any means, without the prior written permission of the author.

Printed and bound in the United Kingdom

This book is sold subject to the conditions that it shall not, by way of trade or otherwise, be lent, re-sold, hired out, or otherwise circulated without the publisher's prior consent in any form of binding or cover other than that which it is published and without a similar condition including this condition being imposed on the subsequent purchaser.

arima publishing
ASK House, Northgate Avenue
Bury St Edmunds, Suffolk IP32 6BB
t: (+44) 01284 700321

www.arimapublishing.com

Acknowledgements

Versions of 'Thunderstorm', 'Her Last Hour on Earth', 'Black Ice and 'Pebbles in the Bucket' have previously appeared in *Poetry Now* publications.

Contents

The Priory of St Anthony	8
And So	9
Thunderstorm	10
Black Ice	11
Two O'Clock in the Morning	12
Mooghaun Castle	14
Kerry	15
Black Cat	17
La France Profonde	18
Urban Vixen	19
Magpies	20
Surveillance	21
Denizens	22
Visitor	23
Miller's Dale	24
The Monsal Trail	25
Macrocarpa Memorial	26
Lullington	27
Squirrel	28
Flight	29
Car Park	30
Train	31
In Winter	32
October	33
Swan	34
Christine	35
Pebbles in the Bucket	36

Her Last Hour on Earth	37
That One Time	38
Menagerie	39
Suffolk	40
The Purple Bus	41
Warehouse	42
The Haberdashers	43
Guy Fawkes'	44
Injury	45
Canine	46
Lounger	47
Parliament	48
November	49
Enigma	50
Fact	51
A Pedestrian, Crossing	52
An Enemy in the Garden	53
The Secret Garden	54
Turbanned	55
Holkham Piggery	56
The Firmament	57

N'es-tu rien qu'une boule,
Qu'un grand faucheux bien gras
Qui roule
Sans pattes et sans bras?

Are you nothing more than a ball,
Than a great fat harvestman
Rolling along
Without legs and without arms?

Alfred de Musset, 'Ballade a la Lune'/'Moon Ballad'

The Priory of St Anthony

The glow of old gold
through the plain glass
of a simple, ancient church
turned those clumsy, hand-knit animals
in a cardboard crib
into gilded, soft-hued icons
- a hierophant's delight -
those dewy, soft-eyed darlings
of the Byzantine rite.

Meantime, outside,
the streets were peopled by crowds
who had long ago,
in consternation and acrimony,
divorced their souls.

They lived under grey and sullen skies,
though all the while above them reigned,
in crimson and purple and blue,
propitious as the Danube, the Tiber
or the Venetian lagoon,
a firmament full jubilant,
enthroning the Goddess,
that most precious moon.

And So

At night,
rain driving on the windscreen,
then fog, a puffball round the moon,
obscures the line of flight.
Velocity imprisoned
in the absent light.

In a garden by the wayside
a bonfire hissing smoke.
Flames, cast leeward by the wind,
burnt orange, pierce the aura
of the street illumination.

Then sudden, lunatic surmise:
a gas attack or suicide!
Oh terror of the saturated kind,
in these strange and feral,
soup primeval, snake-tongued times.

Thunderstorm

A thunderstorm in the street,
a fog of water, grey and fleet,
rain ricochets off smooth-tiled roofs,
car tyres whoosh, then falter,
in the flooded, cambered grooves
and the traffic flow keeps on the move.

Then ear-splitting, renegade laughter
erupts in the dim afternoon
as stoned with astonished release,
in polyphone, lunatic shrieks,
alarm djinns let out of their coops
careen through the air in gambolling loops,
box-hermits, ganged-up,
at last on the loose.

Black Ice

On a nondescript February morning
nineteen people walk the streets like itinerant ghosts.
The twentieth, a pallid girl of twenty-four,
with a wedding planned within year or two
and children, God willing, sometime after,
skewed her car on black ice, broke her neck
and was pronounced dead on arrival,
leaving her colleagues, well,
much as you find them.

Two O'Clock in the Morning

She has a roar like a foghorn
and often plays air-guitar
between the streetlights,
when her chip punnet is empty,
she can't find her key,
she knows we're watching
and he refuses to come downstairs
to let her in.

One morning, at two o'clock,
she told the neighbourhood
she could not get the lock to work:
her key was too big to do any
effing good.

He is older
(she might have been a child-bride
or a concubine)
and shrunken to a scale-model
of the creature he once was.
You hear scratching at the door,
and a palsied whimper
when it's his turn
to be let in.

Last night they woke me up,
for the first time together
and in the company of friends:
a square and portly individual
and an older, leaner,
whippet-faced comrade.

Of course,
I didn't hear everything they said.
In speech which was slurred and indistinct
they mourned the pear tree and the apple boughs
that they had burned as logs
after the bungalow next door was razed
to builders' brown,
together with its long-time orchard ground.

And then the wizened one took his portly soulmate
by the hand
and retreated to the garden shed
from which both, a minute or two later,
emerged,
the portly one clasping an armless, headless trunk,
shakily, to his chest.

I swear by my sleep-struck, clouded eyes
I saw a tipsy, jocund God the Father
hoist the torso of the True Cross.

Since then, I think they are Essenes across the road,
clandestine guardians of exactly who knows what
at searing, mostly fragile, cost.

Mooghaun Castle

Hot and swarming in Summer,
in the Winter, sunken in mud,
beyond the crumbling, dry stone wall at its edge,
some times a grazing bull,
other times hazy, somniferous sheep,
thus the Quarry Wood.

On the left, a septic tank,
grey and roughshod, ensconced
behind a steep and man-made bank,
to sluice the lavatories
in the foursquare Norman keep,
with hybrid roses in its cottage garden
and a textbook bottle-green half-door,
something after *The Quiet Man*
or a Kodakcolour tourist brochure.
In all, a class of Western parador,
the honour of which,
on good days and bad,
gyrates on the slate-roofed parapet
in an Irish-American's Tricolour flag.

Kerry

Monty Murphy was a farmer who drove a tractor
on his way to and from the creamery.
It may have been the only tractor in the village
at the time.
At two, I dubbed him Kerry –
God knows why.

Black Cat

Someone,
who understood
there was a heart ready to be broken,
laid your carcass on the pavement,
with its eyeless socket on the pillow side,
noting in your upturned ear
the gleam of silken sheets,
their easy, uxorious allure.

No other wound below,
a coat untarnished,
in the tender hours
forlorn upon the road.

And even so.

In someone's home,
in unlit corners,
for days and weeks,
for months to come,
unbidden snatches of your absent form
will bind themselves,
like shadows,
to a heart
which has no fortune
but to mourn.

La France Profonde

As the trees in this heartland grow older
the earth moves away,
exposing their grime-cracked, febrile roots,
like teeth in the aged jaws
of those for whom death is near.

Any traveller can see them,
from any passing train,
on the arid ridge above the town;
their crown and leaves abstemious,
their heads bent,
calamitous,
on the crystal air beyond the clouds.

Urban Vixen

She got as far as head and shoulders
out of the gate,
and then she saw me
coming against her,
so she turned tail
and watched me hesitate.

I did my obeisance
and she lifted her head,
finding it curious,
that a human specimen
should greet her,
in daylight
and majesty,
as an old friend.

Magpies

First only one
with his feathers tucked in,
his collar turned up,
standing
in a carpark
in the horizontal rain.

Then another came
and he nipped and tucked
at the plumage of her neck,
- as if for all the world
he was ridding her
of a tribe of undetectable nits.

She stood there
and preened for him as if she liked it:
as if they couldn't have absconded into deepest cover,
in this hailstorm,
in this winter,
in this wet.

Surveillance

A black-and-white she-cat,
spine arched
against a yellow garden wall,
clocks with a lazy, almond eye
the morning office flow;
a brylcreemed magpie,
glinting in the noonday sun,
stands, on sentry guard,
at his watchpoint
on a flapping line of clothes;
a pastel, see-though worm
twists from the steaming summer soil
and thwarts the screen-dazed footfall
of the work-tired
ambling slowly home;
a tattered, hoarse-coughed vixen
snuffles through the hedgerow for food
or trinkets for her young,
to jar the dreams of sleepers
in and out of doors.

Denizens

Two drakes like snails
on a steep grass bank,
enamelled Ottoman turbans
richly-coloured,
in green and blue,
symmetrical,
as if drawn by masters
blinded by decades of ritual practice
and inner meditation
on the forms of their art,
a placid duck between them,
the three rolled up in the knot
of a Celtic brooch,
the clasp of a beak
tucked in the armpit
of each topside wing
unseals the beginning
and the end.

Visitor

A town fox
in my garden,
sniffing at the lush vegetation
of a monsoon Autumn,
the eggshells and the pigeons' wings
left by himself as markers
for intruders
or the bloodline of his nation.

Miller's Dale

Little, baby, fluffy ducks
so far from conceivable human fodder
that their proud-as-punch mother
urged them from the water
to nose round my supine trainers
and see for themselves
this big, white, twin-columned prey.

All five snuffled obediently,
with excitable amber beaks,
at the platform of those feet.

Then off they set, quite sated, quite fleet,
to the reed-bank of feathered repose,
their brisk, bustling mother
shuffling them all back indoors.

The Monsal Trail

The valley was hewn in two
to thread a steam train on a viaduct through
and link the North West to the Capital.

The view from the carriages was as they promised:
spectacular,
blasted,
as it was,
for the paying passenger.

Anyone walking the land,
shoeless,
unable to find a job or enough to eat,
beheld the entire world in catastrophic defeat.

Macrocarpa Memorial

Oblong holes in the bark
where the timber is dead
filled with rhomboid planks
from other companions,
long felled.

Nail heads oxidised
run rust along the grain
of the planted invaders.
Manifold trunks reach down
to where bark meets lawn,
and the bole is fenced round
with seating and plaques
to the human departed.

Here two currents compound,
though to the uninitiated eye,
the dog-walkers in the fields passing by,
it's just a gnarled old tree
in a picturesque country cemetery.

Lullington

Around a curve in the road
lay the surprise of Lullington.

A farrier, working from an unmarked, dark-blue
    transit van,
shoeing one chestnut beast
with an outraged, equine companion
looking uneasily on,
his hindquarters arched towards that labouring man,
tawny and golden in the evening sun.

'You're having a laugh, mate,
if you think you're going to nail one of those
metallic doughnuts
to me.'

Thus yoked, like his friend,
to the wall of the cottage on that bend,
he reared up in anger a futile, recalcitrant head.

Squirrel

A tiny grey squirrel,
eyes too big for an aquiline head,
not enough time in apprenticeship spent
among mortals
and their motorised means,
nibbling on seeds,
eyeing the transient humans
in various states of déshabille,
in the coat he himself would wear
for the whole of his life,
in the middle of the parkland road on which,
inevitably, it seemed,
he would shatter the heart
of his sciurine maker,
and, unseen by the driver,
die.

Flight

At half past four in winter
the buildings on the horizon
turn briefly to gold,
if there has been sun.

A rustle of starling flight
and the Georgian window pane
is dark with the weight of feathers,
three storeys high.

Birds and workers
file off home,
and the invernal evening
ceases to fade.

Car Park

In the saffron light
of an off-site, long-stay car park,
voyagers returning at night
are charmed into speech
by the vulpine creature
lapping pilchards
from a cast-off, oblong tureen.

They have seen
a tarmac fisher queen
at her midnight feast
in a forest of automobiles.
And so, they affirm to each other,
who have not spoken until now,
that this too,
happily,
is a place of wonder.

Train

Little brick-built outhouses,
like solid garden sheds,
on odd bends of the track,
leading to buttressed embankments
decked in pine-needles, dandelion puffs
and coppery leaves -
perennial ghosts from Christmas.
On either side, slatternly dwellings
with domino extensions,
gardens clogged with human detritus:
split wardrobes, burst fridges, draylon settees,
derelict tableaux in the vast longeurs
before the Tottenham North Curve,
moving through Kentish Town on the slow line,
towards the silken djinn-palace
that is our destination:
the lake isle of St Pancras-Kings Cross.

In the evening, as we return,
the moon, like a soft, smoked brie,
pendant over Tesco's.

A month ago, an identical face
over the City end of the Strand,
benevolent at the Griffin-guarded edge:

the Aldwych, as seen by Pepys,
or, later, those silk hats toasting G&S
at the purpose-built Savoy.

These days, the *Chicago* crowd emerges,
part of a grand tradition,
in faux guignol or elasticated jeans,
mostly, though not all,
oblivious.

In Winter

A walk down the hill at eight,
the swish of cars on the boulevard,
the jolt of trains passing at speed,
the drone of planes easing in to land,
the squirrels and pigeons and magpies
all gone, obedient, to bed.

The noise of the engines, it seems,
so much more pronounced,
now the world has turned to black and grey
and darkness is stretched
on the halogen tentpoles of absent day
and the long forbearance of night.

October

At four in the afternoon
the black, moss-green of the lake
and the ducks' webbed feet
pedalling below a surface
in vitreous mosaic.

Enveloped in turquoise and grey,
the sun in its gauzy clouds,
resplendent for five minutes more,
when sketch-lines in smoky filigree
fade in on the charcoal shore.

Then peacocks start kicking their heels
high up in the bouncing branches of the trees,
the birds on the edge of the stream,
the livestock in the fields,
each with an accustomed grace
curls up in an habitual place.

And the humans are left to sidle off home,
to their concrete lairs,
their cream leather sofas,
their large TV screens,
their remote controls.

Swan

A swan stepped out on the road,
a monarch in a flat cap
flailing a stick at the oncoming traffic,
determined to make the heedless flow
acknowledge the years he had lived
before cars were even thought of.

We stopped and waited,
beguiled by an obstinate anatid
the colour and consistency of snow.

When he made it to the other side,
we let out our clutches
and the line wound on,
through rolling, wooded hills,
the vehicles swaying
along the slow cadence of tilt,
in a hint of afterglow.

Christine

> In memoriam Christine Hanbury (1873-1962),
> Hylands House, Essex.

Every year of three,
to sit or stand within the close hedge
and breathe the high haze of Summer,
I've paid homage to her love and grief
in that private garden.

After she died,
twenty years outliving her son,
surrendered to war,
forty years her husband,
his youth spent before she knew him,
her house fell to rack and ruin.

Now, her likeness in the renewed library:
flaxen-haired in oriental crêpe-de-chine,
smiling on those who walk her park,
tread her onetime public rooms,
trippers all, but few of whom
discern the musky damask rose
of such a woman's time in bloom.

Pebbles in the Bucket

Puffed up like a barn owl,
crested, tufted, replete
with a season's worth of nourishment
in only a couple of weeks,
a coat as smooth and downy as silk,
a gaze as solid and trusting
as teak.

Purring, huffing,
like pebbles in the bucket,
a million of them all at once
in leathery, croaking unison;
through an amber bellows,
the sweet-scented aroma
of paw-tufts, cat-food and leaves.

Her Last Hour on Earth

Her elfin face was squared in resignation.
It was the look of those who knew
they were, presently, to die.
From her, it was a parting gift.
It willed her home from the road:
up the drive, behind the garage,
through the hedge, along the lawn,
in the cat-flap, across the kitchen floor
and down, finally, behind the sofa,
with no use of her hind legs
and her spine irrevocably broken;
all her tiny, delicate, internal parts
crushed to putrefaction,
but no mark on her tortoiseshell coat.
She glanced at me and sighed as she landed.

All this as a last gift,
commanding to the end:
she would not have me figure out,
in ignorance and desperation,
how she took her parting breath.

That One Time

I broke the unbreakable truth
the night she died.

I stared straight into her eyes,
lowered myself to the edge of the surgery table
before the sedative
and the lethal narcotic
stopped her stalwart life.

That one time.

And she wanted to remain at home.
In peace. Behind the sofa.
Within the privacy of her own eyes.
Inviolate.

But I, in my panic,
cast out all the rules.

Menagerie

A china menagerie deep like a crib:
beasts from the jungles, the plains of Africa,
the icecaps, even the Steppes;
king among them an orange giraffe:
soft brown eyes, lollipop ears, macaroon nose,
amid the tall grass and sundry exotica.

At peace, at pasture, in pampas,
curator of an imagined time,
a childhood, a haven, a respite,
from non-cute,
cargo-bearing,
post-initiation rite
life.

Suffolk

In memoriam Eileen Barker.

You promised me horizons.

In aged company,
I glimpsed them from a car.

Luminous clouds and golden sheets of light,
and chaff and dust and wheat.

Now the weatherman says Autumn is due,
though winter has long dawned in the back seat,
and solstice cannot now be far.

The Purple Bus

A leaf the colour of rolled tobacco,
the consistency of charred paper,
the size of its own life,
falls in the slipstream of the purple bus
as it rounds a bend.

It is not yet Autumn,
just an unfortunate leaf
fallen to an early iteration
in the Summer breeze.

Warehouse

The moon like Mae West,
doe-eyed in the sky,
loitering,
with Dianesque intent,
round the smoking remains
of a glassless silhouette,
razed, that night,
in silence,
to the ground.

The Haberdashers

On the corner of a square in Bologna,
a proper, old-fashioned haberdashers
with several assistants,
each knowing exactly their business,
climbing stepladders to retrieve goods
from the high wooden shelves,
all the way up to the ceiling,
scaffold-high and queasy.

Guy Fawkes'

The sky is clouded,
rain obscures the light
and damps reverberations -
the stentorian crash
of fairground-coloured lights
propelled from every second minuscule back garden
towards the stoic vault at night.

Cats, convinced that this is aerial bombardment,
cower behind sofas, under chairs,
in the secret places in the blankets at the bottom of
    the bed,
as if to lay themselves, in readiness, in earth.

They think if they cannot see skywards,
those fizzing payloads will not catch them unawares,
and each lull in the bombing pattern overhead
finds one or two emerging,
dulcet-throated, ready to be fed.

But yet, amidst their human minders,
not flinging paint-balls at the cobwebbed night
are some, who, in a hundred feline lifetimes,
will never split asunder
gunpowder, trauma, blight.

Injury

A useless back paw
sweeping the floor,
echoes of another night
and another tortoiseshell paw
almost inanimate
as she dragged herself across the wood.
This time, it's only a minor ache,
a muscle pulled, a claw snagged
in a shadow fight
with a fleece-wrapped fist
and blithe, unthinking, human might.

Canine

A curl of white by her bowl.

I thought it was an extra-long nail,
a flourish of calligraphy left for me
on the cold, grey tile.

Instead, it had a rotten brown root
below a perfectly-formed corner tooth,
forever separated now
from the bottom left side
of a rosebud mouth
which closes still in a perfect wow,
to sound
the honeyed miaow.

Lounger

If you leave the past too long
it will pixellate and die.

That fox, brown fox, scrawny fox
in the morning sun
bronzing himself,
will fade into the undergrowth,
though he lay stretched
full pelt
on a tan-worshipper's
man-made, fibre-meshed
sunbed.

Parliament

That assemblage of cats
gathered in the other world,
like Aztec empresses
with their quetzal feathers
all in a line.
Each has reigned for a decade
or a lustrum of my life,
observed and kept counsel,
bequeathed a set of habits
and expectations,
which each successor
has disappointed, outstripped
or undermined,
as I strove each time
for the meek compliance
of the sight-unseen
child bride.

November

A fox,
the wraith of one I once knew,
darted across the road
in the dark,
in the wind,
in the spots of rain,
in a gap between the headlights,
nearly translucent,
only on two planes,
malnourished
far beyond the threshold
of recognisable pain.

Enigma

In the grass
it seemed an impossibility,
a goose's neck, quiescent
or a wooden handle,
severed.

And then it leapt
and proved to be a squirrel,
dancing nose to tail
with another juvenile.

Fact

Bison, the European sort,
are the answer to forest fires.
Their ordure is sweeter on the land
than sheep or cattle pats.

They thin out the pines
so the sun shines through
and twenty-four species
can thrive anew.

This provides the glue
that keeps the soil on the land,
the moisture in the plants,
and fire from taking hold.

Herds of bison to the north of St Tropez:
a sight to make many a paparazzo's day.

A Pedestrian, Crossing

A vixen like a cheetah,
a bit too thin for comfort,
the fur too bleached, unkempt,
dashed across the road,
legs at full stretch
like a shiny Stubbs thoroughbred.

Only inches from my headlights.

I saw the decision to leap,
gauged against the oncoming speed.

Maybe she knew I was an old friend
and would not touch her
with the bonnet of a car
that was also red.

An Enemy in the Garden

In every life,
a day like this one comes,
a harbinger of doom.
In her case,
on a sunny October afternoon.

An enemy in the garden.
One with no furnishings to see,
no swinging gut to show the years
like rings round the heart of a tree.

She charged out, squared up,
one third of the way from the house
to the wind-sown boundary shrubs.

But she was the one to tilt her head,
sideways and to the left,
she was the one to turn around,
stepping as if on spiders' webs,
surrendering the ground.

The enemy took another triumph
lightly. One of many left in store,
until one day she too meets the ignominy
of yielding at her own back door.

The Secret Garden

A cloistered garden of cosy brick walls
where passers-by are invited in,
in daylight hours between nine and five,
to watch the prey birds duck and dive
and the little ones save their skins.

The gardener champions canna lilies
and the beds are a riot of colour,
above all in the summer
when there's time to dream
of how it might have been,
to be resident of such a house,
in celluloid collar or high-neck blouse,
with tennis in corsets on the lawn,
amusing oneself from dusk to dawn:
such frivolous colts, such thoroughbred fillies,
gambolling, on the brittle edge of doom.

Now there's a wicker man
recumbent on the boarded-over well.
He wears his whalebones
on the outside,
in reverie, a century on
from the plunging hellhole of the Somme.

Turbanned

The banana trees are encased in their gilded cages,
with bluer than cobalt, cube-pleated domes,
armour against the sleet, the wind and the snow,
while all about them petals, stems, leaves and hedges
uncaparisoned, like cannon fodder in the open,
await the onslaught of fog and rain and frost,
drawing gruel only from attenuated sun,
while the ordinary hardy trunks go on and on.

The shorn bananas stand safe within the turban fold,
like medieval knights encamped in pointed tents,
wintering out, playing chess against the cold,
parlaying battle with their enemies amongst the
    clouds,
though all too cumbersome and obsolete to joust,
squared mummies, wrapped in forage-padded
    shrouds.

Holkham Piggery

One was warned not to step off the rough gravel path
onto the scraggy grass,
though there was no fence,
onto the terrain of those myriad rosy-pink pigs
and their sideways bean-tin, khaki-green,
wartime sheds.
It would be a danger to health
- far likelier theirs than ours.

The day was taupe,
the landscape greenish flat,
the air close clammy and the swine
suede luminous.

Across the moat, the foremost stood
and boldly dogged my stare,
caste breeding arming her
contemptuous,
Churchillian,
on the limen of a word-of-honour,
spell-bound lair.

The Firmament

Easy to forget, the importance of the sky,
at night, when it is clear of planes
and other incidental traffic.
When the only passers-by are clouds,
the only lights the stars,
the only face the moon,
in any of its guises.

Tonight it was translucent
on a bed of greenish China blue,
transparent like a porcelain bowl,
for Jasmine tea and the usual ceremony.

The rising, the setting,
you can rely on it,
a point of anchorage,
always there,
even when untraceable to the questing eye.

www.ingramcontent.com/pod-product-compliance
Lightning Source LLC
Chambersburg PA
CBHW061254040426
42444CB00010B/2381